DELTA PUBLIC LIBRARY
402 MAIN STREET
DELTA, OHIO 43515

WITHDRAWN

JUN 1 8 2014

Women in Medicine

Major Women in Science

WOMEN IN ANTHROPOLOGY

WOMEN IN CHEMISTRY

WOMEN IN ENGINEERING

WOMEN IN INFORMATION TECHNOLOGY

WOMEN IN MEDICINE

WOMEN IN PHYSICS

WOMEN IN SPACE

WOMEN IN THE ENVIRONMENTAL SCIENCES

WOMEN INVENTORS

WOMEN WHO BUILT OUR SCIENTIFIC FOUNDATIONS

MAJOR WOMEN IN SCIENCE

Women in Medicine

Kim Etingoff

Mason Crest

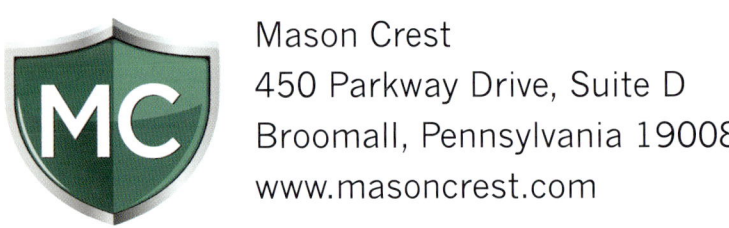

Mason Crest
450 Parkway Drive, Suite D
Broomall, Pennsylvania 19008
www.masoncrest.com

Copyright © 2014 by Mason Crest, an imprint of National Highlights, Inc. All rights reserved. No part of this publication may be reproduced or transmitted in any form or by any means, electronic or mechanical, including photocopying, recording, taping or any information storage and retrieval system, without permission from the publisher.

Printed and bound in the United States of America.

First printing
9 8 7 6 5 4 3 2 1

Series ISBN: 978-1-4222-2923-1
ISBN: 978-1-4222-2929-3
ebook ISBN: 978-1-4222-8898-6

The Library of Congress has cataloged the
　　　hardcopy format(s) as follows:

　　　　　Library of Congress Cataloging-in-Publication Data

Etingoff, Kim.
　Women in medicine / Kim Etingoff.
　　　pages cm. -- (Major women in science)
　Audience: 12.
　Audience: Grade 7 to 8.
　Includes index.
　　ISBN 978-1-4222-2929-3 (hardcover) -- ISBN 978-1-4222-2923-1 (series) -- ISBN 978-1-4222-8898-6 (ebook)
　1. Women physicians--Juvenile literature. 2. Women in medicine--Juvenile literature. I. Title.
　R692.E88 2014
　610.82--dc23
　　　　　　　　　　　　　2013009824

Produced by Vestal Creative Services.
www.vestalcreative.com

Contents

	Introduction	6
1.	What Does It Take to Be a Doctor?	9
2.	Rita Levi-Montalcini: Nobel Prize Neurologist	15
3.	Irene Ayako Uchida: Understanding Down Syndrome	21
4.	Rosalyn Yalow: Understanding Radioisotopes	25
5.	Marcella Farinelli Fierro: Medical Pathologist	31
6.	Nancy H. Nielsen: President of the American Medical Association	37
7.	Antonia Novello: First Woman Surgeon General	41
8.	Margaret Chan: Director General of the World Health Organization	47
9.	Dale Emeagwali: Cancer Researcher	51
10.	Lori Arviso Alvord: Navajo Doctor	55
11.	Opportunities for Women Today in the Field of Medicine	59
	Index	63
	About the Author & Picture Credits	64

Introduction

Have you wondered about how the natural world works? Are you curious about how science could help sick people get better? Do you want to learn more about our planet and universe? Are you excited to use technology to learn and share ideas? Do you want to build something new?

Scientists, engineers, and doctors are among the many types of people who think deeply about science and nature, who often have new ideas on how to improve life in our world.

We live in a remarkable time in human history. The level of understanding and rate of progress in science and technology have never been greater. Major advances in these areas include the following:

- Computer scientists and engineers are building mobile and Internet technology to help people access and share information at incredible speeds.
- Biologists and chemists are creating medicines that can target and get rid of harmful cancer cells in the body.
- Engineers are guiding robots on Mars to explore the history of water on that planet.
- Physicists are using math and experiments to estimate the age of the universe to be greater than 13 billion years old.
- Scientists and engineers are building hybrid cars that can be better for our environment.

Scientists are interested in discovering and understanding key principles in nature, including biological, chemical, mathematical, and physical aspects of our world. Scientists observe, measure, and experiment in a systematic way in order to test and improve their understanding. Engineers focus on applying scientific knowledge and math to find creative solutions for technical problems and to develop real products for people to use. There are many types of engineering, including computer, electrical, mechanical, civil, chemical, and biomedical engineering. Some people have also found that studying science or engineering can help them succeed in other professions such as law, business, and medicine.

Both women and men can be successful in science and engineering. This book series highlights women leaders who have made significant contributions across many scientific fields, including chemistry, medicine, anthropology, engineering, and physics. Historically, women have faced barriers to training and building careers in science,

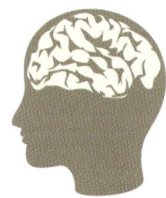

which makes some of these stories even more amazing. While not all barriers have been overcome, our society has made tremendous progress in educating and advancing women in science. Today, there are schools, organizations, and resources to enable women to pursue careers as scientists or engineers at the highest levels of achievement and leadership.

The goals of this series are to help you:

1. Learn about women scientists, engineers, doctors, and inventors who have made a major impact in science and our society
2. Understand different types of science and engineering
3. Explore science and math in school and real life

You can do a lot of things to learn more about science, math, and engineering. Explore topics in books or online, take a class at school, go to science camp, or do experiments at home. More important, talk to a real scientist! Call or e-mail your local college to find students and professors. They would love to meet with you. Ask your doctors about their education and training. Or you can check out these helpful resources:

- *Nova* has very cool videos about science, including profiles on real-life women scientists and engineers: www.pbs.org/wgbh/nova.
- *National Geographic* has excellent photos and stories to inspire people to care about the planet: science.nationalgeographic.com/science.
- Here are examples of online courses for students, of which many are free to use:
  1. Massachusetts Institute of Technology (MIT) OpenCourseWare highlights for high school: http://ocw.mit.edu/high-school
  2. Khan Academy tutorials and courses: www.khanacademy.org.
  3. Stanford University Online, featuring video courses and programs for middle and high school students: online.stanford.edu.

Other skills will become important as you get older. Build strong communication skills, such as asking questions and sharing your ideas in class. Ask for advice or help when needed from your teachers, mentors, tutors, or classmates. Be curious and resilient: learn from your successes and mistakes. The best scientists do.

Learning science and math is one of the most important things that you can do in school. Knowledge and experience in these areas will teach you how to think and how the world works and can provide you with many adventures and paths in life. I hope you will explore science—you could make a difference in this world.

Ann Lee-Karlon, PhD
President
Association for Women in Science
San Francisco, California

Introduction

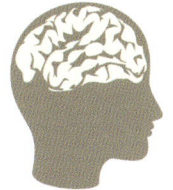

What Does It Take to Be a Doctor?

Ask a group of young people today what they want to be when they grow up, and you'll probably find at least one or two who say, "A doctor." Being a medical doctor is the dream of many students today, and it can be an achievable one for many.

The road to becoming a doctor is a long one. Practicing medicine requires dedication, hard work, and even some sacrifices along the way. Yet thousands of people make the decision to start that journey.

In the past, if you were a woman, becoming a doctor was especially difficult. The medical profession used to be made up almost entirely of men. A woman who wanted to practice medicine was considered unusual, and she faced many obstacles to her success.

Nonetheless, many women decided to follow their dreams. They overcame the adversity they faced. Today, it is easier for women to become doctors, and more and more women are entering this field.

Why Be a Doctor?

There are many reasons why someone would choose to become a medical doctor. A common reason is to help people or take care of them. Doctors do good in the world, and many young people want to be a part of that. They imagine the thrills they would get from curing someone of cancer, or delivering a baby into the world.

Other young adults are fascinated by the human body. Perhaps they're even fascinated by one body system or organ in particular. People who want to study the heart might become cardiologists, while people who are interested in reproduction might become gynecologists. Becoming a doctor is the best way to study human **anatomy**!

Many doctors come from families with doctors in them. They grow up seeing their mother or father (or both!) work as a doctor, and it becomes a normal choice for a profession later on in life. They have always wanted to be a doctor, and already know a little bit about what it's like.

Some people might say that doctors chose their jobs because they wanted to make money. That might be true for some doctors, but it's not the end of the story. Doctors-in-training have to go to years and years of school and go into debt before they ever start making money. Most people need to have another good reason to go through the tough training it takes to become a practicing doctor. Money isn't the only one!

Education

Doctors spend between eleven to sixteen years in school before they are allowed to practice medicine independently. That is a long time to follow your dream.

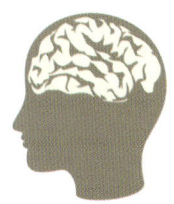

As a medical student, you will have opportunities to interact with patients, as well as do labwork. You will also work with more experienced doctors.

First, those interested in becoming doctors must get a bachelor's degree. It doesn't usually matter what the major is, but many students choose a science-related degree like chemistry or biology. Some colleges and universities also offer pre-med courses and programs for those students who are sure they want to go on and become doctors.

The next step is medical school. Candidates must have good grades, recommendations, and experience. They also have to take the Medical College Admission Test (MCAT). Medical school programs are four years long. The first two are spent mostly in class. Students learn about anatomy, **pharmacology**, how to examine patients, and much more. Classes require a lot of work, since students are learning valuable skills that will affect people's lives!

The last two years of medical school are on-site, meaning that students work with patients. They **rotate** through different departments, such as **internal medicine**, **pediatrics**, and psychiatry. Rotations help students decide what they want to focus on for their career.

What Does It Take to Be a Doctor?

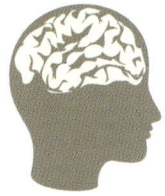

After medical school, potential doctors must complete a residency. Students choose a specialty, then start to get experience during a residency at a hospital. They aren't independent doctors yet, but they are gaining the practical knowledge they need to be doctors.

Finally, people who have completed their medical residency must get licensed. Besides finishing their education, they have to pass tests before they can really become a doctor. In the United States, students take the United States Medical Licensing Exam (USMLE). Only then can you become a full doctor.

Character

Education is only one part of being a doctor. Besides the skills and knowledge doctors learn during school, they need to have certain qualities in order to be successful.

Doctors have to be good problem-solvers. They won't always know what is wrong with a patient, or how to fix it. Every doctor needs to be creative and good at solving problems to give patients the best care. It doesn't hurt to be a thoughtful risk-taker either, since many treatments will require some risks.

Good doctors should also have some people skills. Whether telling patients' families that their loved one has a serious disease or giving someone a routine checkup, doctors interact with people all the time. They'll be better at their jobs if they are good at communicating and being **empathetic**. Good people skills mean better care and more comfort for the patient.

These are just a few of the things involved in becoming a doctor. Women have always had the character and intelligence it takes to become a doctor, and today, more and more women are achieving success in the field of medicine. Successful women doctors show the way to girls who are thinking about this career path.

Words to Know

Anatomy: The structure of the body or body parts of a living thing.
Pharmacology: the study of how drugs and medicines interact in the body.
Rotate: take turns filling different roles.

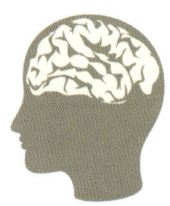

Internal medicine: the branch of medicine that focuses on the treatment and prevention of adult diseases.
Pediatrics: the branch of medicine that treats children.
Empathetic: understanding others' feelings.

Find Out More

American Medical Assocation, "Requirements for Becoming a Physician"
www.ama-assn.org/ama/pub/education-careers/becoming-physician.page.

Heller, Tania. *On Becoming a Doctor: Everything You Need to Know about Medical School, Residency, Specialization, and Practice.* Chicago: Sourcebook, 2009.

MomMD, "Why Become a Doctor?"
www.mommd.com/whybecome.shtml.

U.S. Bureau of Labor Statistics, "Occupational Outlook Handbook, 2012–2013 Edition, Physicians and Surgeons"
www.bls.gov/ooh/healthcare/physicians-and-surgeons.htm.

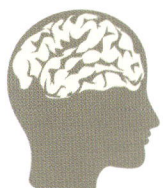

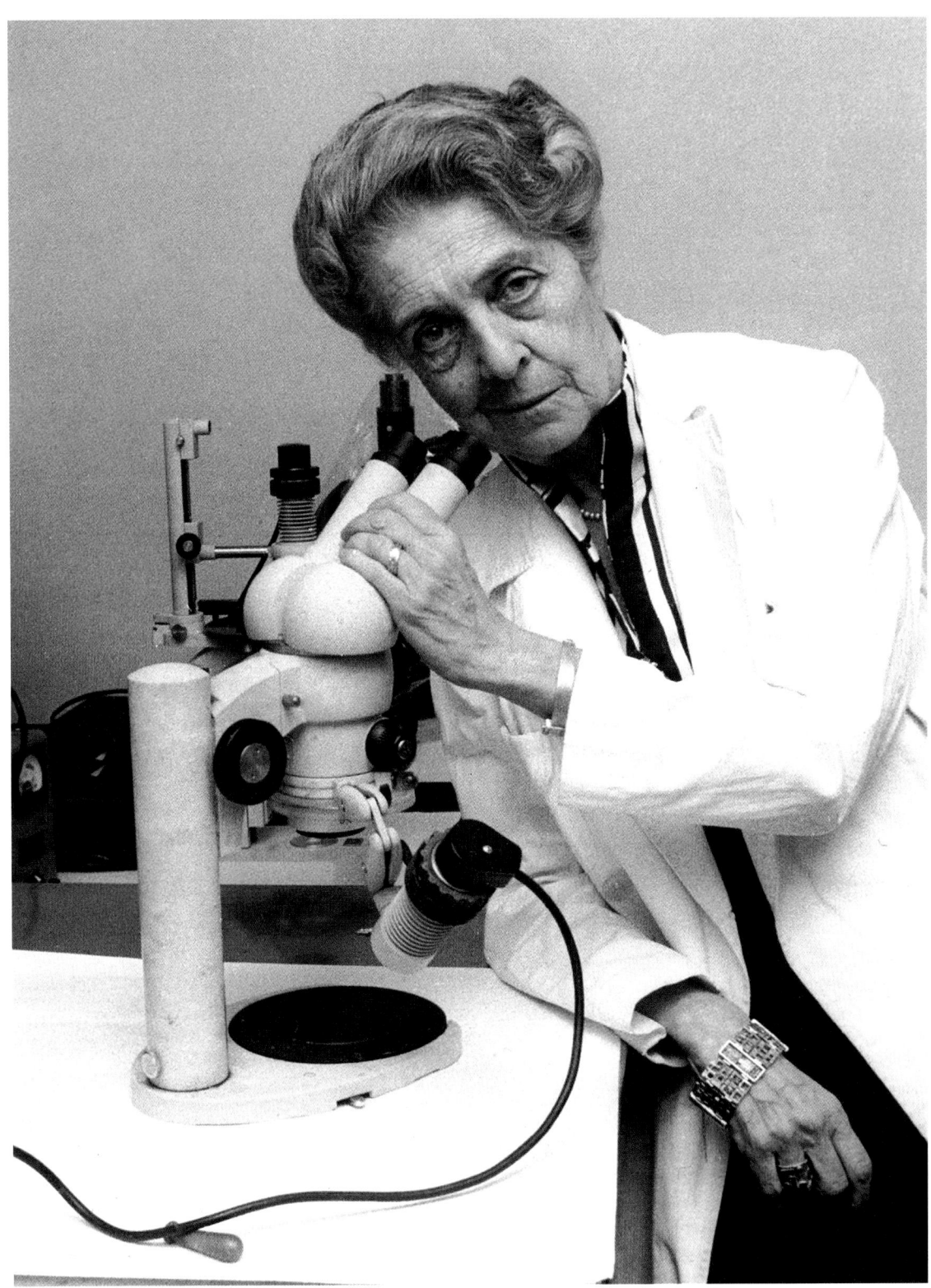

Rita Levi-Montalcini:
Nobel Prize Neurologist

2

I talian-born Rita Levi-Montalcini had to fight sexism and the horrors of World War II to achieve her dream, but that dream would one day bring her a coveted Nobel Prize.

Rita and her twin sister Paola were born in Turin, Italy, on April 22, 1909, the third and fourth children of Adamo Levi, an engineer and mathematician, and Adele Montalcini, an artist. Adamo and Adele instilled in the girls and their older siblings a love of learning. But though Rita's father believed education was

Rita as a young girl in Italy.

important, he had his limits as to what he considered to be an "acceptable" education for women. Like many men of his time and place, Adamo believed that a woman should not be educated in areas that would encourage her to have a career that might take away from her obligations as a wife and mother. Rita and her sisters were encouraged to study art and literature rather than math or science, and there was no talk of the girls attending college.

Rita's sisters had no problems with their father's rules. Rita, however, was not content with the roles women were expected to fill in Italy in the the 1920s and '30s. She wanted more, and she was able to convince her father to let her expand her education. Rita began taking classes in math, Latin, and Greek. When she graduated from high school, she enrolled in University of Turin Medical School. There, she studied and worked with Giuseppe Levi, beginning the study of nerve growth that would eventually lead to her Nobel Prize in Physiology or Medicine.

Rita graduated from medical school in 1936 with a degree in medicine and surgery. She chose to specialize in **neurology** and psychiatry, and she enrolled in a three-year program to continue her education. But in 1938 her education and career took a detour, as Benito Mussolini, the Italian leader, began his campaign to rid Italy of Jews. That year, the "Manifesto per la Difesa della Razza" ("Manifesto in Defense of the Race") was issued. Signed by prestigious leaders in many scientific areas, including zoology, physiology, biology, and anthropology, the **manifesto** proclaimed there was one pure race, the Aryan race, and that all others were inferior. They further claimed that this had been proven scientifically.

The following year, Mussolini's government passed a law that removed all non-Aryan and Jewish individuals—including Rita—from any professional positions. She briefly went to Brussels, Belgium, at the invitation of a neurological institute there. Just before the German Army invaded Belgium in 1940, Rita returned to her family home in Turin. There, she set up a research laboratory in her bedroom to study nerve growth in chick embryos. Giuseppe Levi, with whom she had studied during medical school, joined her in her research, inspired by an article written by Viktor Hamburger in 1934 about the surgical removal of limbs from chick embryos.

In 1941, Allied forces bombed Turin, heavily damaging the city. Rita, her family, and her laboratory moved to a cottage in the Piemonte countryside. Two years later, the German Army invaded Italy, and Rita and her family went to Florence, where they remained, living in hiding, until the Allies liberated the area in 1944.

When Florence was safe once more, Rita went to work as a doctor in a refugee camp there. She treated injuries as well as many infectious diseases, such as typhus. When the war in Italy finally ended in 1945, Rita and her family returned to Turin, and she returned to the medical school.

Rita and Giuseppe Levi published the findings of the research they had conducted on chick embryos during the war. It came to the attention of Viktor Hamburger, who had spurred Rita's interest in the subject. At the time, he was the chairman of the Zoology Department at Washington University in St. Louis, Missouri. In 1947, he invited Rita to come to the university to teach and continue her research. The plan was for her to stay for a year at the most. The results of her research, however, were so successful that Rita stayed in the United States.

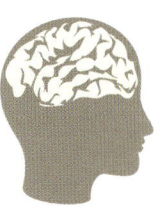

At Washington University, Rita began working with **biochemist** Stanley Cohen. During the 1950s, their research focused on nerve growth, particularly what regulated nerve growth. Rita's discovery of nerve growth factor, which stimulates nerve growth, and their research in what promotes cell growth, added important tools in the study of cancer, **dementia**, and birth defects. In 1986, Rita and Stanley were awarded the Nobel Prize in Physiology or Medicine.

The Nobel Prize

The Nobel Prize in Physiology or Medicine is awarded once a year for outstanding discoveries in the fields of life sciences and medicine. It is one of five Nobel Prizes established in 1895 by Swedish chemist Alfred Nobel, the inventor of dynamite, in his will. It is one of the most famous and respected prizes in the world. As of 2011, 102 Nobel Prizes in Physiology or Medicine have been awarded to 199 men and 10 women. In the years ahead, as more and more women become doctors, women will be catching up with men, though.

Rita remained at Washington University, eventually rising to full professorship. She became a U.S. citizen in 1956, but she never gave up her Italian citizenship. She established a research facility in Rome in 1962, traveling between the two countries to do her work. In 1969, she accepted the position of director of the Institute of Cell Biology of the Italian National Council of Research in Rome, which she held until 1978.

Besides the Nobel Prize, Rita received many awards in recognition of her work. In 1968, she became the tenth woman elected to the United States National Academy of Sciences. In 1983, she, Stanley, and Viktor Hamburger were awarded the Louisa Gross Horwitz Prize from Columbia University. In 1986, the same year they won the Nobel Prize, Rita and Stanley received the Albert Lasker

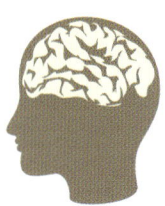

Award for Basic Medical Research. The following year, Rita was given the National Medal of Science, the highest honor in the scientific world in the United States.

When she retired from Washington University in 1977, Rita returned to Italy and continued her work there. But in 2001, she embarked on another career path: politician. She was appointed senator for life by then Italian president Carlo Azeglio Ciampi. Rita's political positions were not always favorably received by her fellow senators or by members of the general public. Some bloggers resorted to insulting her because of her age and Jewish heritage. Still, Rita continued to participate in government matters—when they didn't conflict with her educational programs throughout the world.

Words to Know

Neurology: the study of nerves.
Manifesto: a document that tells the public the views or intentions of the writer.
Biochemist: a scientist that studies the chemical makeup of living cells.
Dementia: decreased memory, judgment, and concentration, often accompanied by personality and emotional changes, caused by damage to the brain's neurons from disease or trauma.

Find Out More

Levi-Montalcini, Rita. *In Praise of Imperfection: My Life and Work*. Trans. by Luigi Attardi. New York: Basic Books, 1989.

Rita Levi-Montalcini: Autobiography
nobelprize.org/nobel_prizes/medicine/laureates/1986/
levi-montalcini-autobio.html.

Spangenburg, Ray. *Rita Levi-Montalcini: Seeking the Secrets of Growth*. New York: Facts on File, 2009.

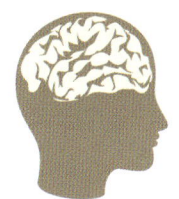

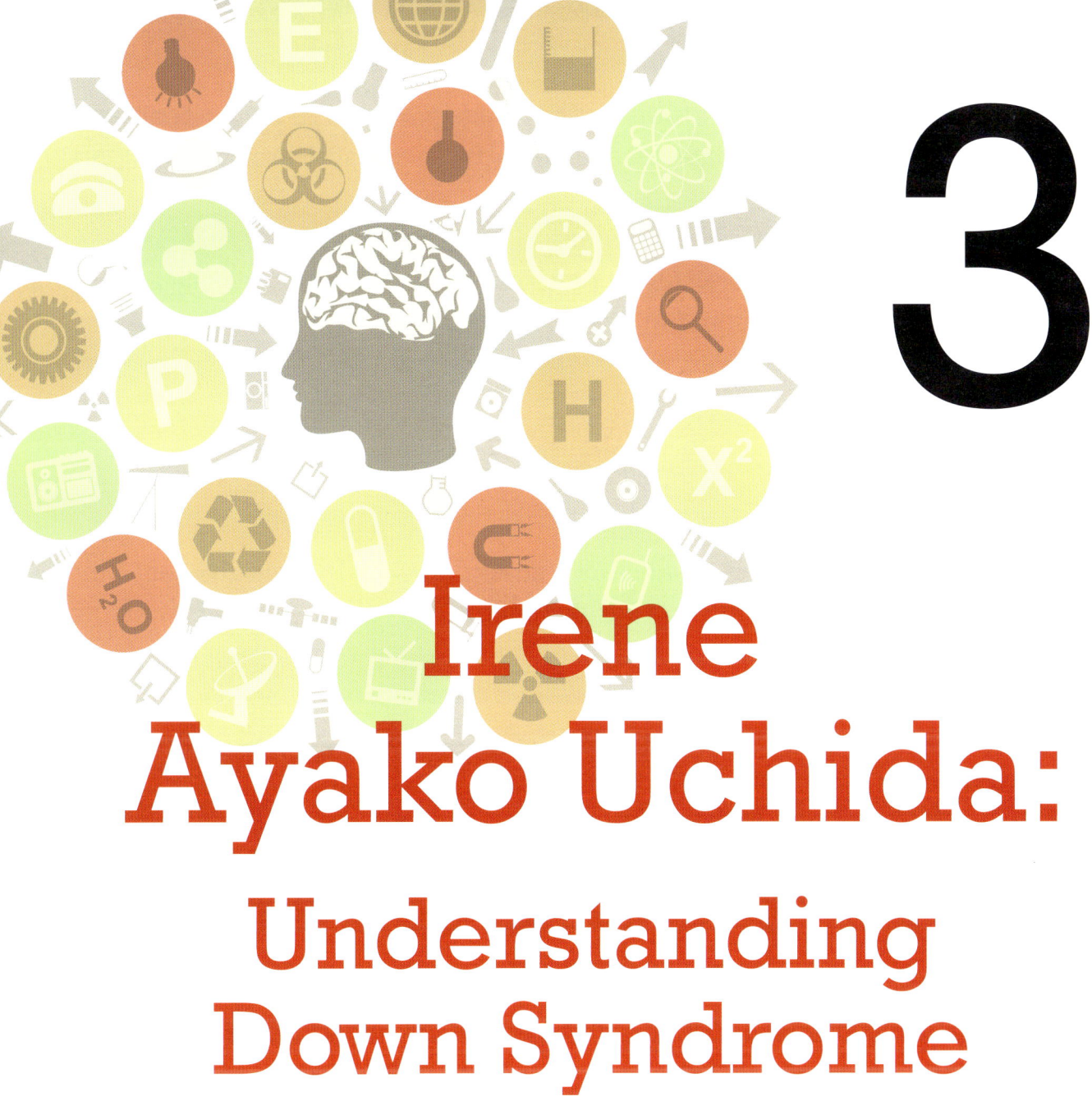

3

Irene Ayako Uchida:
Understanding Down Syndrome

One of Canada's most important scientists didn't even plan to become a scientist. In fact, her path of discovery was not easy.

Ayako Uchida was born on April 8, 1917, in Vancouver, British Columbia, one of five children of Japanese-born parents. A piano teacher gave her the name Irene, because she had difficulty pronouncing Ayako. After she graduated from high school, Irene enrolled in the University of British Columbia. She studied English literature for two years. In 1941, Irene interrupted her education to join her mother and sisters in Japan. Only Irene was able to leave Japan and head back to Canada before Japanese forces attacked Pearl Harbor, Hawaii, on December 7.

The next few years were ones of upheaval for Irene and her family. Japan's attack on Pearl Harbor had been a surprise. Fear ran rampant, especially among those living on the Pacific Coast of the United States and Canada, nearest to Japan. Many Americans believed that it was only a matter of time before Japan attacked again.

Fear of more violence led to drastic measures in Canada and the United States. Many officials and members of the general public worried about the Japanese population of North America. Some believed resident Japanese could be plotting an attack from the inside. Government officials thought the best way to handle the situation was to move resident Japanese to **internment camps**. In 1942, Irene was relocated to one of those camps, along with several thousand other resident Japanese. Many, like Irene, had been born in Canada, but that made no difference. For many Americans and Canadians, the fact that people had Japanese blood was enough to make them a threat to the country.

Irene was moved to an internment camp at Christina Lake in British Columbia. When camp officials found that she had been to college, they asked her to serve as principal of a camp school in Lemon Creek, British Columbia. She accepted the position and was sent to Lemon Creek.

In 1944, Irene was finally able to continue her education. The United Church gave her a place to stay and provided financial support for her to attend the University of Toronto. Two years later, she earned a bachelor's degree in social work. Irene planned on continuing at Toronto to earn a master's degree in social work. But a discussion with some of her professors changed her mind. They suggested that she study **genetics**. Eventually, Irene went on to earn a doctorate in human genetics in 1951.

After completing her doctoral program, Irene went to work at the Hospital for Sick Children in Toronto. There, she conducted research on twins and children with Down syndrome, a disease characterized by mild to moderate intellectual disabilities, short stature, and distinctive facial characteristics.

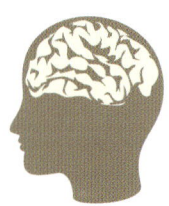

In 1960, Irene became the director of the Department of Medical Genetics at Children's Hospital in Winnipeg, Manitoba; she also had a teaching appointment at the University of Manitoba. In Manitoba, Irene continued her research into Down syndrome. She wanted to find out if there was a connection between prenatal exposure to radiation—primarily through X-rays of the mother's abdominal region—and the development of Down syndrome. Through her studies, Irene found that there was a connection between the mother's exposure to abdominal X-rays and birth defects in future pregnancies. It is now known that Down syndrome is caused by an extra chromosome 21, which can come from the father or the mother.

Research and Being a Doctor

Not all doctors work with patients. Some medical doctors work in scientific labs in universities and companies. They work to discover and develop new treatments for diseases. Because of medical research, people today live longer and healthier lives than ever before.

In 1970, Irene founded the **Cytogenetics** Laboratory at McMaster University in Hamilton, Ontario. By then, her reputation had grown extensively, both within and outside of Canada. Many organizations sought her out for her expertise. These included the American Society of Human Genetics, the Science Council of Canada, the Advisory Committee on Genetic Services for Ontario, the American Board of Medical Genetics, and the Canadian College of Medical Geneticists.

Irene also received a number of awards, including Women of the Year, Winnipeg, 1963; Woman of the Century 1867–1967 for Manitoba, 1967; 1000 Canadian Women of Note from 1867–1967, 1983; and the Founder's Award from the Canadian College of Medical Geneticists, 1995. In recognition of her work, Irene was made an Officer of the Order of Canada in 1993.

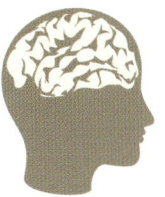

After leaving the Cytogenetics Laboratory, Irene became professor **emeritus** in the Department of Pediatrics and Pathology at McMaster University, continuing to focus her research on Down syndrome and birth defects.

Words to Know

Internment camps: detention centers often used for members of certain nationalities or ethnic groups during a war.

Genetics: the study of genes, the hereditary material found in cells.

Cytogenetics: the branch of biology studying cell structure, chromosomes, and heredity.

Emeritus: when a person keeps the honorary title of professor even though they are retired.

Find Out More

Irene Ayako Uchida
www.science.ca/scientists/scientistprofile.php?pID=21&pg=0

Karnes, Frances A. and Kristen Stephens. *Young Women of Achievement: A Resource for Girls in Science, Math, and Technology*. Amherst, N.Y.: Prometheus Books, 2002.

Shell, Barry. *Sensational Scientists: The Journeys and Discoveries of 24 Men and Women of Science*. Vancouver, B.C.: Raincoast Books, 2005.

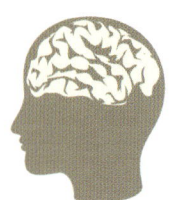

4

Rosalyn Yalow: Understanding Radioisotopes

I n the 1930s and 1940s, it wasn't always easy for a woman to get the education necessary to follow certain careers. Some women gave up and settled for something less than their dream. Not Rosalyn Yalow. She became both a physicist and a doctor, two careers where few women in her day could succeed.

Rosalyn Sussman was born in New York City on July 19, 1921. Her mother, Clara, came to the United States from Germany when she was four years old. Simon Sussman, Rosalyn's father, was born on New York City's Lower East Side, home to many Eastern European Jewish immigrants.

Like many people of the time, neither Clara nor Simon had a high school education. They were determined that Rosalyn and her older brother, Alexander, would go to college, so they encouraged educational activities in their home. Rosalyn learned to read when she was young, but the family could not afford many books. Every week, Alexander and Rosalyn visited the public library to check out books.

During elementary school, Rosalyn learned to love math. When she entered seventh grade, she began her love of chemistry. After Rosalyn graduated from high school, she enrolled in Hunter College, an all-girls' school affiliated with the City University of New York (the school has since enrolled boys and girls). Though she still enjoyed math and chemistry, her attention turned to physics. Physics was very much in the news during the 1930s. Eve Curie's biography of her mother, Nobel Prize-winner Marie Curie, was published in 1937. In 1939, when Enrico Fermi gave a lecture at Columbia University about his discovery of nuclear fission, Rosalyn attended. The more she found out about physics, the more certain she was that this was the field for her.

Despite the inroads women had made in the science professions, it was still not easy for women to find spots in graduate programs in physics, let alone jobs in the field. Concerned about their daughter's future, Rosalyn's parents encouraged her to become an elementary-school teacher. They need not have worried, although Rosalyn's entry into a physics graduate program wasn't quite the usual one! When she graduated from Hunter in January 1941, she went to business school to study **stenography**. One of her physics professors had arranged for her to become a secretary to a biochemist at Columbia, but first she had to learn stenography. He assured her that this "backdoor method" was likely the easiest way for her to get into the graduate program.

Fortunately for Rosalyn, she only had to stay in stenography school for about a month. In February, she was offered a teaching assistantship in physics for the following fall at the University of Illinois, Champaign-Urbana. In the meantime, she continued working as a secretary, but without stenography.

In September 1940, Rosalyn moved to Illinois. She quickly found herself the only woman in the College of Engineering. There had not been a woman in the program since 1917. Except for a few classes, Rosalyn had never been in a class

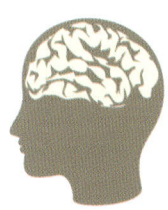

26 **WOMEN IN MEDICINE**

with men. Now, she was the only female in a class full of men. Rosalyn found that her physics background was lacking compared to her classmates, so she sat in on undergraduate courses to bolster her knowledge. Rosalyn's hard work during her first year paid off. She received all A's and an A–.

What's an Assistantship?

Many colleges and universities help graduate students by giving assistantships. If you get an assistantship, you will usually help professors with their responsibilities as either teaching assistants or research assistants. Rather than receive hourly wages, students often get a stipend that offsets some or all of their tuition. Assistantships provide much needed experience for graduate students, increasing their future employment options.

After the Japanese attacked Pearl Harbor, Hawaii, in December 1941, Rosalyn's already full schedule got busier. Though many of the male students in her classes left to work on projects in other places, members of the army and navy came to Illinois for training. Rosalyn balanced a heavy teaching load and her own research and courses with her 1943 marriage to fellow student Aaron Yalow, whom she met her first day on campus; the couple would have two children. In January 1945, Rosalyn received a doctorate in nuclear physics. She went to work for a Federal Telecommunications Laboratory in New York and waited for her husband to complete his thesis. In 1946, Rosalyn accepted a teaching position at Hunter College. Many of her students were returning veterans.

In 1947, Rosalyn accepted a part-time consultant position with the Bronx Veterans Administration Hospital. She helped the hospital equip and develop a **radioisotope** service while still teaching at Hunter. Three years later, Rosalyn left Hunter and went to work full time at the hospital. In July 1950, Solomon Berson came to work with Rosalyn, thereby establishing one of the most successful teams in radioisotope research.

Rosalyn told an interviewer: "They told me that as a woman, I'd never get into graduate school in physics, so they got me a job as a secretary at the College of Physicians and Surgeons and promised that, if I were a good girl, I would take courses there." Instead, Rosalyn went on to become the second woman to win a Nobel Prize in medicine.

The primary focus of Rosalyn and Solomon's research concerned the use of radioisotopes in determining blood volume, in diagnosing thyroid diseases, and in studying the metabolism of iodine. By 1959, they had developed radioimmunoassay, a radioisotope tracing method by which tiny quantities of various biological substances in the blood can be measured. At first, the method was used to measure insulin levels in people with diabetes. Since then, it has been used to trace small quantities of other hormones and enzymes. Though their discovery could have made Rosalyn and Solomon a great deal of money, they refused to **patent** the method.

In 1968, Solomon left to assume the chair of the Department of Medicine at Mount Sinai School of Medicine. He died four years later. At Rosalyn's request, the laboratory where they had worked was renamed the Solomon A. Berson Research Laboratory.

Rosalyn became a research professor in Mount Sinai Hospital's Department of Medicine in 1968. Later, she would be named the Solomon Berson Distinguished Professor at Large.

Her work has brought Rosalyn many awards. In 1975, she and Solomon received the AMA Scientific Achievement Award. In 1976, she became the first female recipient of the Albert Lasker Award for Basic Medical Research. The following year, she received the Nobel Prize in Physiology or Medicine, together with Roger Guillemin and Andrew V. Schally. Because he had died in 1972, Solomon could not share the award. In 1988, Rosalyn received the National Medal of Science.

Words to Know

Stenography: the art of writing rapidly in shorthand.
Radioisotope: a radioactive isotope of an element.
Patent: a government license that allows only the creators of an invention to make, use, or sell that invention for a specific amount of time.

Find Out More

Rosalyn Yalow, Assaying the Unknown
pubs.acs.org/subscribe/journals/mdd/v04/i09/html/09timeline.html.

Straus, Eugene. *Rosalyn Yalow: Nobel Laureate: Her Life and Work in Medicine*. New York: Basic Books, 2000.

Waisman, Charlotte, and Jill Titejen. *Her Story: A Timeline of Women Who Changed America*. New York: Collins, 2008.

Women of the Hall, Rosalyn Yalow.
www.greatwomen.org/component/fabrik/details/2/174.

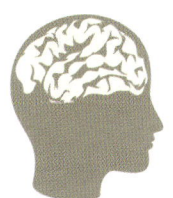

5

Marcella Farinelli Fierro: Medical Pathologist

When Marcella Farinelli Fierro became the chief medical examiner of Virginia, many people in the United States and elsewhere knew her. But they didn't always know that a literary character many had grown to love was later based on Marcinella and her work.

Marcella Farinelli was born in 1941. When Marcella was very young, her father died after a five-year battle with a brain tumor. Her mother was only in her thirties when Marcella's father died and left her with two young daughters. Though money was scarce, Marcella's mother vowed that her daughters would receive a good education.

Marcella loved school, especially her science classes. In elementary school, while the other students ate their lunches and played, Marcella would read the science teacher's books. She also enjoyed reading adventure stories, ones that opened her imagination to the possible.

In 1962, Marcella graduated from D'Youville College in Buffalo, New York, with a degree in biology. Marcella had been interested in medicine since her father's illness, but female physicians were rare as she was growing up. Though there were not many role models, Marcella knew she wanted to be a doctor, and she enrolled at the State University of New York at Buffalo. In 1966, she received her doctor of medicine degree in **forensic pathology**.

After graduation, Marcella completed her internship and residency requirements at the Ottawa Civic Hospital in Ottawa, Ontario, Canada. She completed an additional pathology rotation at the Cleveland Clinic Education Foundation in Ohio. She moved on to Virginia Commonwealth University, becoming chief resident in pathology. Her work brought her a **fellowship** in forensic pathology at the Medical College of Virginia at Virginia State University in Richmond from 1973 to 1974. Marcella eventually earned **board certification** in anatomic and clinical pathology. In 1994, she was named chief medical examiner for Virginia.

What Does a Chief Medical Examiner Do?

A chief medical examiner is a coroner, a government official who confirms and certifies the death of an individual within a jurisdiction. A coroner may also conduct or order an investigation into the manner or cause of death, and investigate or confirm the identity of an unknown person who has been found dead within the coroner's jurisdiction.

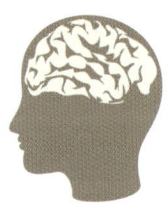

WOMEN IN MEDICINE

A pathologist uses a variety of tests to diagnose diseases. A forensic pathologist uses many of the same tests to determine the cause of death—and if a crime has been committed, these tests may offer clues as to who committed the crime and how.

Besides her work as a medical examiner, Marcella has spent a great deal of time helping prepare the next generation of medical examiners. She has taught at the Medical College of Virginia at Virginia Commonwealth University since 1973. For more than thirteen years, she taught clinical pathology at the University of Virginia, Charlottesville. Marcella served on the staff of the Medical College of Virginia Hospitals in Richmond from 1975 to 1992. Beginning in 1983, she also served as a consultant to the Federal Bureau of Investigation (FBI) in the area of body identification. Marcella also provided expert testimony on behalf of a bill that would change laws regarding the killing or malicious wounding of a pregnant woman.

Marcella Farinelli Fierro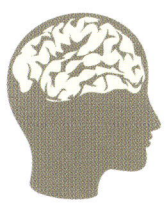

Marcella is active in maintaining the **professionalism** of pathology, especially forensic pathology. Since 1979, she has been on the board of editors and acted as a reviewer for the *American Journal of Forensic Medicine and Pathology*. Marcella has also written many articles and is a frequent lecturer and presenter at conferences and meetings of professional and academic organizations.

Marcella sees her role as a forensic pathologist as an opportunity to help the living as well as solve the mysteries of death. She does mortality reviews, which study a death and then develops a **protocol** that can be used to prevent future deaths from the same cause.

The general public's exposure to pathology has grown dramatically over the past several years. Marcella has had a role in that process as well. She was featured in an episode of *New Detective*, a television series on the Discovery Channel. The series shows how people use science to get justice for the victim and his or her family.

Many readers "know" Marcella, though, through a series of immensely popular books written by Patricia Cornwell. In the early 1980s, Patricia went to work in a medical examiner's office, where Marcella was among her coworkers. What Patricia really wanted to be was a mystery writer, however. She plugged away, collecting rejection slip after rejection slip. Marcella helped her, encouraging Patricia and tirelessly answering her questions. In 1988, Patricia completed her first book starring Dr. Kay Scarpetta, a medical examiner. Patricia has made no secret of the fact that the character who made her a well-known—and very successful—author is based on Marcella. In 2008, Patricia published her sixteenth book featuring Dr. Scarpetta.

Although Marcella has had a busy professional life, she has also managed to have a full personal one as well. She and her husband, Robert, a gynecologist, have two children. Marcella enjoys going to the opera and theater and reading.

Marcella retired as Virginia's chief medical examiner and as a professor at the Medical College of Virginia in 2008, but she hasn't left the field entirely. Marcella continues to advance the field of forensic pathology by teaching at the Virginia Institute of Forensic Science and Medicine and at Virginia Commonwealth University.

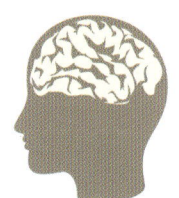

Words to Know

Forensic pathology: the branch of medicine used for legal matters or solving crimes and concerned with determining the cause of death and examination of injuries.

Fellowship: a grant by a university or other institution given for advanced study, often in a specialized subject.

Board certification: the process by which a person is tested and approved to practice in a specialty field of medicine.

Professionalism: the skill and capability expected of a professional in their field of study.

Protocol: an established code of procedure and conduct.

Find Out More

Changing the Face of Medicine, Dr. Marcella Farinelli Fierro
www.nlm.nih.gov/changingthefaceofmedicine/physicians/biography_111.html.

Wilson, Jacque, "The Monster Patricia Cornwell Created," CNN.com www.cnn.com/2008/SHOWBIZ/books/12/15/patricia.cornwell.scarpetta/index.html#cnnSTCText.

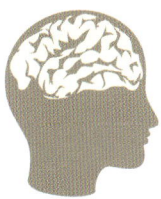

6

Nancy H. Nielsen:
President of the American Medical Association

Today, most people don't think twice when a woman doctor enters an examination room. Women have refused to be restricted to medical specialties that treat women only, such as gynecology, obstetrics, or pediatrics. Women doctors can now be found practicing in all medical areas. In fact, the American Medical Association reports that in 2003–2004, female medical school applicants outnumbered male applicants for the first time.

Though women doctors are now commonplace, men still dominate many areas of medicine. The field's largest organization, the American Medical Association (AMA) elected its first female president, Nancy Dickey, in 1998. In 2008, Nancy H. Nielsen, MD, PhD, was elected as the second female president and the 163rd president of the AMA.

Nancy Nielsen earned a doctorate in **microbiology** from Catholic University of America in Washington, D.C. Though she thought about going to medical school, she put those plans on hold. Then, after she gave birth to her fifth child, Nancy decided it was time to pursue her goals. She was twenty-nine years old when she enrolled in the University of Buffalo School of Medicine and Biomedical Sciences in Buffalo, New York. In 1976, she received her medical degree and earned board certification as an **internist**.

Nancy developed an interest in infectious diseases. Over the years, she honed her expertise in the field. She became a popular lecturer on infectious diseases, as well as on nutrition and other health issues.

Besides being a practicing physician in Buffalo, New York, Nancy became an active member of many professional organizations. She became the first woman to be president of the medical and dental staff at Buffalo General Hospital and the first woman president of the Erie County Medical Society. She served as a chief medical officer for the Western New York office of the New York State Department of Health. Nancy also served as an officer of the Medical Society of the State of New York and of the New York State Society of Internal Medicine. She is also a senior associate dean for medical education and a clinical professor in the University of Buffalo School of Medicine and Biomedical Sciences.

Nancy became involved with the American Medical Association in 2000. She served three consecutive terms as vice speaker of the association's House of Delegates, the branch that establishes the group's policy positions, and four consecutive terms as speaker. She served two terms on the Council of Scientific Affairs. In that capacity, she helped develop AMA policy on public-health issues such as alcoholism in women and colorectal cancer screening recommendations. Nancy also represents the association to outside groups.

In her inaugural address, Nancy stressed the importance of an improved health-care system in the United States:

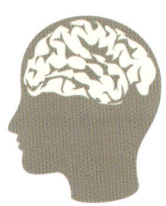

We must use our profession's **inherent** commitment, courage, and compassion to come together with patients, employers, and insurers to build a bridge that provides safe passage across the health care chasm. Physicians know the barriers to health care reform better than anyone. We must be the engineers who design [an]. . . American solution for a better health care system.

She hopes that the American Medical Association and its members—especially medical educators—can play important roles in shaping the health-care system:

The task of today's medical educator is to prepare the next generation of physicians to be advocates for their patients, activists for reform, scientifically prepared, **ethically** driven, and optimistic about the future of our profession. . . .

As we prepare to pass the torch to the next generation of clinicians, researchers, and educators, we must also prepare our students to take charge of crafting the solutions for our sick health care system. ... Let's "cure" our health care system and teach our students to care about doing so as well.

After her term as AMA president, Nancy served as senior advisor to the Center for Innovation within the Center for Medicare and Medicaid Services in Washington, D.C. In 2009, Nancy was elected a member of the Institute of Medicine (IOM) of the National Academy of Sciences. IOM membership is considered one of the highest honors in the fields of health and medicine. Nancy has certainly demonstrated all that a woman doctor can achieve!

Words to Know

Microbiology: the branch of biology concerned with microscopic organisms.
Internist: a professional that specializes in internal medicine.
Inherent: having to do with an inseparable or permanent part of something's identity.
Ethically: acting in agreement with the accepted principles of right and wrong.

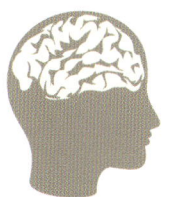

Find Out More

Chin, Eliza Lo. *This Side of Doctoring: Reflections from Women in Medicine.* New York: Oxford University Press, 2003.

Nancy H. Nielsen, MD, PhD
www.ama-assn.org/ama1/pub/upload/mm/37/bio-nielsen.pdf.

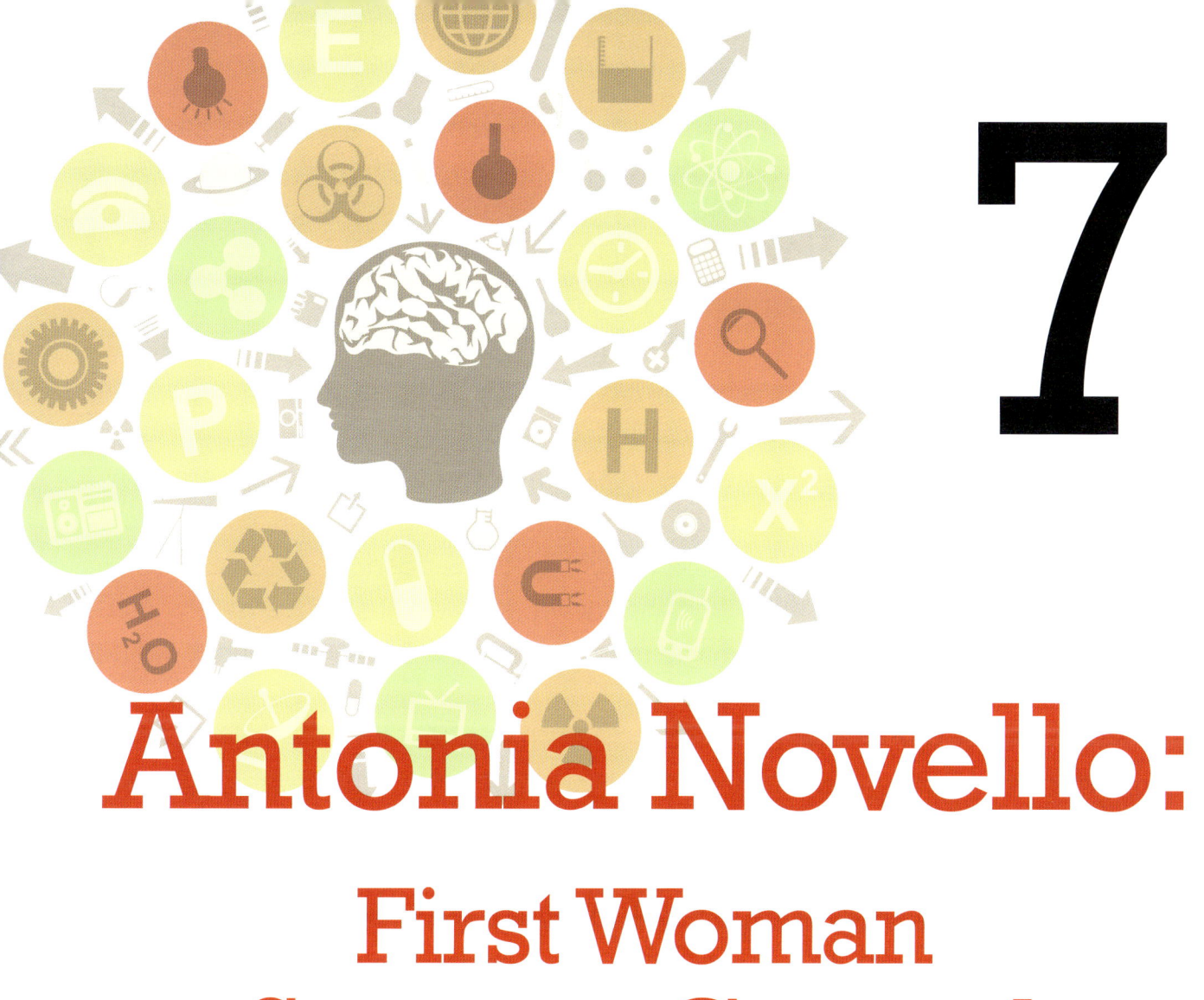

7

Antonia Novello:
First Woman Surgeon General

I n the mid-1940s and 1950s, a little girl growing up in Puerto Rico had serious health issues. Little did she know at the time, but the strength she gained from dealing with them would help make her the person who would become the number-one public health official in the United States.

Antonia Coello was born in Fajardo, Puerto Rico, on August 23, 1944. She was born with **congenital** megacolon, a condition in which nerve cells are missing in the intestines, meaning that her body had trouble moving digested material through her system.

Antonia was born into a middle-class family. Her father died when she was eight years old, and her mother was the driving force in the family, even after she remarried. When Antonia was in junior high school, her mother was the principal and sometimes her teacher. From an early age, Antonia knew that her mother was going to make sure she got a good education.

When Antonia's mother became the high-school principal, she selected all Antonia's teachers. She would even switch a teacher's class responsibilities to make certain that Antonia had the best teachers, regardless of what grade she was in. Some of Antonia's classmates questioned whether she got the grades because she earned them, or because of her mother's influence. Already feeling like an outsider because of her medical issues, this added to Antonia's sense of loneliness. But rather than let it get her down, she was just more determined to succeed. And she used humor to be accepted. She was active in most of the school's clubs and had many friends.

Antonia was also determined to prove that the grades she received were no fluke—nor were they evidence of her mother's influence. She graduated from high school shortly before her sixteenth birthday and entered the University of Puerto Rico at Rio Piedras. When Antonia was eighteen and attending college, she had surgery to correct her intestinal condition. (Surgery to correct complications from this surgery had to be performed four years later.) She didn't let it delay her education, though; Antonia received a bachelor's degree in 1965.

After graduation, she enrolled in the University of Puerto Rico School of Medicine in San Juan. Antonia had known she wanted to be a doctor since she was a small child. After all, she had spent a lot of time surrounded by health-care professionals. They were some of her most important role models.

When Antonia graduated from medical school in 1970, she accepted an internship and later a residency in **nephrology** at the University of Michigan Medical Center in Ann Arbor. In 1970, she also married navy flight surgeon Joseph Novello, who later became a well-respected psychiatrist.

After she completed her residency, Antonia accepted a fellowship in internal medicine at the Medical Center. She then moved on to the Department of Pediatrics at Georgetown University School of Medicine, where she had a fellowship as well. Following her residency at Georgetown, Antonia went into private pediatric practice in Virginia.

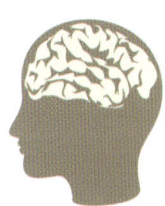

WOMEN IN MEDICINE

In 1978, Antonia thought about joining the U.S. Navy, but a recruiter discouraged her because she was a woman. Instead, she joined the Public Health Service Commissioned Corps. Her first assignment was at the National Institute of Arthritis, Metabolism and Digestive Diseases at the National Institutes of Health (NIH). She moved through several positions at the NIH and rose through the officer ranks. In 1986, she became the Deputy Director of the National Institute of Child Health and Human Development (NICHD). While at the NICHD, Antonia developed an interest in AIDS research, especially in pediatric AIDS.

Throughout her career, Antonia was a master at multitasking. In 1982, she balanced her work at the NIH with getting a master's degree from the Johns Hopkins School of Hygiene and Public Health. As a member of the U.S. Senate Committee on Labor and Human Resources, Antonia played a major role in the creation of the Organ Transplantation Procurement Act of 1984.

On March 9, 1990, President George H. W. Bush appointed Antonia to the Surgeon General post, making her the first woman and first Hispanic in that office. In her role as Surgeon General, Antonia was responsible for determining the country's health priorities. She focused most of her attention on health issues of children, women, and minorities. She tackled underage drinking and smoking and was very critical of tobacco companies' use of cartoon characters such as Joe Camel to promote their products.

Careers in Medicine and Politics

You might think that being a doctor and being a politician are two very different careers. But medicine and politics are often intertwined. Politicians help decide which medical issues should be funded. They shape the way a country's money is spent in taking care of its people. Often, doctors become frustrated by their government's control. They want to get involved and help shape the government's decisions about health care and medical research. After all, the doctors are the ones who are the experts in this field! It makes sense that some doctors decide to become politicians.

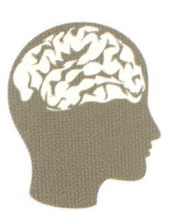

Antonia with New York State governor George Pataki in her role as State Commissioner of Health.

In June 1993, Antonia left the post of Surgeon General. She returned to the Public Health Services and accepted the position of Special Representative for Health and Nutrition at UNICEF. She served in that post until 1996. She became a visiting professor in public health at Johns Hopkins School of Hygiene and Public Health after leaving UNICEF. In 1999, Governor George Pataki of New York named her State Commissioner of Health, a position she held until 2007 when she returned to the Washington, D.C. area and accepted a professorship at Georgetown University.

Antonia's work on behalf of public health issues has not gone unnoticed. She is the recipient of numerous awards and honors, including the Surgeon General's Exemplary Service Medallion and Medal and the National Women's Hall of Fame.

Words to Know

Congenital: a medical condition that has been present since birth.
Nephrology: the branch of medicine dealing with the kidneys, their function, and disease affecting them.

Find Out More

Waisman, Charlotte, and Jill Titejen. *Her Story: A Timeline of Women Who Changed America*. New York: Collins, 2008.

Women of the Hall: Antonia Novello
www.greatwomen.org/component/fabrik/details/2/3.

Yoshizawa, Linda. *Antonia Novello: Doctor for the Nation*. Boston: Houghton Mifflin, 2006.

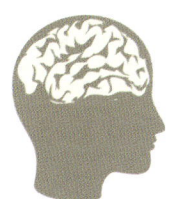

8

Margaret Chan: Director General of the World Health Organization

Margaret Chan helped her homeland deal with two of the most serious health issues in recent history and was put in charge of global health as the leader of the world's biggest health organization.

Margaret Chan Fung Fu-chun was born in Hong Kong in 1947. She attended Northcote College of Education and was qualified to teach home economics. Margaret went on to attend the University of Western Ontario in Canada and earned her bachelor's degree in home economics in 1973. Four years later, she received her medical degree, also from the University of Western Ontario. She received a Master of Public Health degree from the University of Singapore. Margaret also later attended Harvard University Business School.

In 1978, Margaret accepted a position with the government of Hong Kong. As a medical officer, she worked in the world public health. She became assistant director of the Department of Health in 1989, and was appointed deputy director in 1992.

Margaret became the first female to lead Hong Kong's Department of Health in 1994. During her tenure, she had to face two major health crises. In 1997, H5N1 avian influenza (commonly called "bird flu") broke out. In the beginning, poultry farmers were the ones who suffered most. But once it was discovered that the virus could be transmitted between species, people became increasingly frightened they would become infected. As director of the Department of Health, Margaret tried to ease people's fears. She told them she often ate chicken, and they had nothing to fear by consuming poultry products. When the problem turned out to be more serious than originally reported—both in terms of the number of cases and the possibility of a breakout in the human population—Margaret was criticized. She was accused by many of misleading and hiding information about the outbreak from the public.

Many people changed their mind about Margaret and her effectiveness as the leader of the Department of Health when she ordered the killing of approximately 1.5 million infected poultry. Politicians opposed her actions, claiming they would cause a serious economic downturn. When destroying the birds controlled the spread of avian flu, the criticism faded away, however.

Avian flu was not the only health crisis to surface while Margaret headed the Department of Health. In 2003, Hong Kong was hit with an outbreak of severe acute respiratory syndrome—SARS. Almost three hundred people died, and Hong Kong's economy was hit hard. Again, many politicians criticized Margaret, including the Legislative Council of Hong Kong and victims' families. They argued that Margaret acted too slowly and, in some cases, failed to act at all. Many believed that she was too easily swayed by authorities in mainland China into accepting misleading information. The Hong Kong government established a committee of SARS experts to evaluate how the crisis had been handled. They

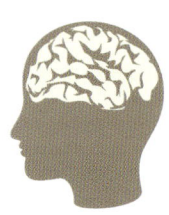

determined that Margaret was not at fault; the problem lay with the Hong Kong health-care system. Because there was little communication between the hospital authority and the public-health administration, information sharing was inadequate.

When Doctors Make Mistakes

Everyone makes mistakes. As hard as people try to be good at their jobs, sooner or later they miss something they should have noticed or they make a wrong decision. If you're a banker, and you make a mistake, it could mean you have to go back and redo the numbers so that people's bank accounts are accurate; if you're a cook, and you make a mistake, your food may turn out tasting really bad; but if you're a doctor and you make a mistake, sometimes people die. This is a hard responsibility to face. If you want to become a doctor, you have to accept that your mistakes will be very serious. You will have to do the best you can and learn from the mistakes you make. That's all anyone can do, in any field.

In 2003, Margaret accepted a position as director of the Department for Protection of the Human Environment of the World Health Organization (WHO). Working through the United Nations, WHO is responsible for providing leadership on global health issues, establishing research priorities, setting standards, and providing technical support to countries. It also watches and keeps track of health trends. She became director of the **Communicable** Diseases Surveillance and Response department and representative of the director-general for **pandemic** influenza in June 2005. In late 2005, Margaret was assistant director-general for communicable diseases.

In November 2006, Margaret was appointed director-general. In numerous interviews, Margaret stated that her primary goals for the WHO included the improvement of the health of Africa's people as well as the improved health of

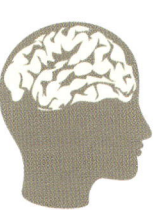

women. She is also concerned about the probability of an influenza pandemic. Margaret is not alone in her concern. Many health experts fully expect a major influenza outbreak, believing the question is when rather than if. Besides the medical preventive and treatment issues that she must deal with, Margaret must also take economic issues into consideration in the plans and actions of the WHO. Margaret believes that her experiences with the avian flu and SARS outbreaks in Hong Kong will be beneficial as she helps steer the WHO in the direction of preventing a pandemic. She knows she has one of the most important jobs in the world!

Words to Know

Communicable: contagious; easily transmitted.
Pandemic: widespread outbreak of a disease over a large area.

Find Out More

Dr. Margaret Chan: Biography
www.who.int/dg/chan/en/index.html.

Emmons, Garry, "One on One with Dr. Margaret Chan," *Harvard Business School Bulletin*
alumni.hbs.edu/bulletin/2006/march/oneonone.html.

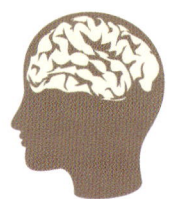

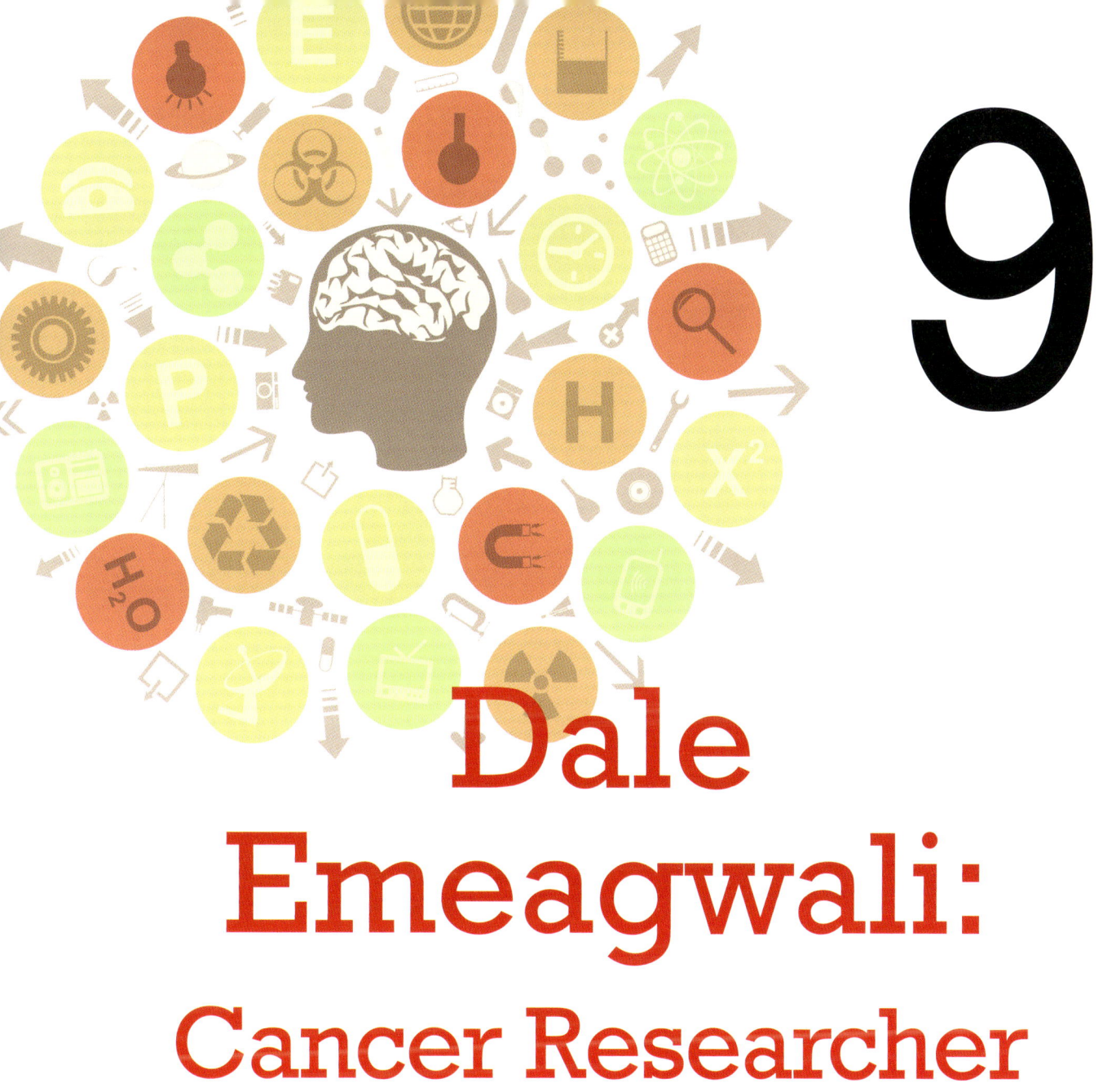

9

Dale Emeagwali:
Cancer Researcher

Growing up, Dale Brown had big dreams. She loved science and wanted to make it her career. Dale turned her big dreams toward the study of things that are very small.

Dale Brown was born on December 24, 1954, in Baltimore, Maryland. Her father, Leon, worked for the *Afro-American*, a newspaper aimed toward the black population of Baltimore and Washington, D.C. Doris, Dale's mother, was a teacher in the Baltimore school system.

Dale says that if you want to be a doctor: "A passion for the subject, a burning desire to answer a question, and an interest in the outcome are essential."

Dale learned early in life that education was important. Her parents encouraged her to study hard, and it paid off; Dale was often at the top of her class. Dale's interest in science began early, with her parents talking to her about science and helping her perform scientific experiments at home. Her parents' enthusiastic support was in sharp contrast to what many black students interested in math and science experienced in school. In an article in *The Science Teacher*, Dale says:

> We were taught inadvertently, and sometimes directly, that we couldn't do [math]. . . . When a Black child said he wanted to be a doctor, he was slapped upside the head and told to stop being simple.

In 1972, Dale graduated from Northwestern High School. After graduation, she enrolled in the historically black Coppin State College in Baltimore, where she decided to major in biology. A course in microbiology, the study of how organisms such as viruses, bacteria, and parasites exist and affect lives, set Dale on her career path.

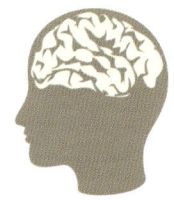

In a 2004 interview in *The Science Teacher,* Dale said that she found microbiology fascinating. She was also attracted to the speed with which she could get results.

Experiments and results are attained quickly with bacteria because they grow at such a rapid rate—they can multiply every 20 to 40 minutes. Often results can be produced the same or next day.

Dale graduated from Coppin State College in 1976. She continued her education at Georgetown University School of Medicine in Washington, D.C. For the first time, Dale was away from her family. The culture surrounding Georgetown University School of Medicine and Washington, D.C., was very different from what she had experienced in her life up until this point. For one thing, most of her classmates at Georgetown were white; at Coppin, they had been black. But Dale was able to fit in, and her academic success continued. She was often at the top of her class here as well. Dale had a goal, and she focused her ambition on accomplishing it.

At Georgetown, Dale concentrated on research in the field of bacteria found in soil. She also studied viruses and **protozoa**. In 1981, she received her doctorate in microbiology. She moved on to the University of Minnesota, where she was a research fellow. There she met computer scientist Philip Emeagwali, originally from Nigeria. They married and had a son, named Ijeoma.

In 1996, Dale received the National Technical Association's Scientist of the Year Award. This award is given in recognition of scientific discoveries that benefit humanity. Dale was honored for her work in cancer research, in particular the discovery that **malignant** tumor growth could be suppressed by inhibiting the **expression** of Ras **oncogene**. Ras is a protein, and the Ras oncogene is the cause of many cancers in humans.

Dale has received many other awards as well, including fellowships from the National Institutes of Health, the American Cancer Society, and the National Science Foundation.

In addition to her work as a scientist, Dale is passionate about being a role model to young people, especially young black students. She remembers the barriers people tried to place in the way of her dream to become a scientist, and

Dale Emeagwali

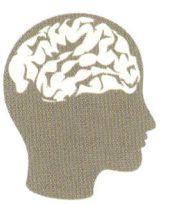

she wants to empower young people to break through obstacles—as she did. Dale's work with young students began when she was a Fellow at the University of Minnesota. With her husband and the staff of the Science Museum of Minnesota, she organized African American Science Day. One of the goals of the project was to show that black people could be successful in science-related careers.

For many years, Dale has taught biology at Morgan State University in Baltimore, Maryland. She also works hard to instill the importance of a good education in students, conducting workshops for inner-city youth to help them feel excited about science.

Words to Know

Protozoa: single-celled organisms that live in water or as parasites inside animals.
Malignant: (in regards to a tumor) cancerous, invasive, characterized by uncontrolled growth.
Expression: production of a protein through the action of a gene.
Oncogene: any gene involved in initiating cancerous growth.

Find Out More

Dale Emeagwali
emeagwali.com/dale.

Marché, Wina. *African American Achievers in Science, Medicine, and Technology: A Resource Book for Young Learners, Parents, Teachers, and Librarians.* Bloomington, Ind.: 1st Books Library, 2003.

Sullivan, Otha Richard. *Black Stars: African American Scientists and Inventors.* New York: Wiley, 2001.

10

Lori Arviso Alvord:
Navajo Doctor

Sometimes, when children are growing up, their career choices may seem limited. Children living in poverty may have a hard time believing they will ever achieve a career that is **prestigious**, pays well, and requires many years of college. As a child, Lori Arviso Alvord certainly had no idea what lay ahead for her.

Lori Arviso was born in 1958 in New Mexico. Her father was Navajo and worked as an electrical technician for the Bureau of Indian Affairs. Her mother, a secretary, was white. Lori was raised on a reservation in Crownpoint, New Mexico, a very small town with a mostly Native American population.

Despite her mixed heritage, Lori has always identified with the Navajo side of her family. After all, that was the culture she experienced every day on the reservation. In addition to the rich spiritual history of the Navajo, Lori also saw firsthand some of the negative characteristics of life on the reservation. Like many reservations, life on the Crownpoint reservation included high alcoholism rates, an inadequate school system, and a sense of hopelessness.

This might have been the way life was, but to Lori, that didn't mean things had to be this way. At least not for her. Neither of Lori's parents had gone to college, and most of the students on the reservation did not attend college—if they even graduated from high school. Lori, though, knew that if she wanted to make a better life for herself, a college education would increase her likelihood of success. So she planned to attend a state college, as most of her college-going classmates did.

A chance meeting changed Lori's plans—and likely her future as well. She met a Navajo student who was attending Dartmouth University in New Hampshire. It was very rare for a Navajo student to attend an **Ivy League** school such as Dartmouth, but Dartmouth was reaching out to Native American students, encouraging them to study there. Lori applied to Dartmouth and was accepted. Acceptance was only the first step in attending however; Dartmouth was—and is—an expensive school to attend. Lori received a small scholarship from her tribe, and she was able to get grants from Dartmouth to help make up the difference.

Lori experienced significant culture shock when she arrived on the Dartmouth campus. Not only was the campus population **diverse**, Lori found that she had many career options available to her. She had entered Dartmouth intending to become a teacher or pharmacist, but, seeing the careers available to her, Lori changed her mind and decided to become a doctor.

Lori's success at Dartmouth affected more than just her and her immediate family. As students back in Crownpoint heard about Lori's experiences at Dartmouth, she became a role model. Other Crownpoint students began to think about going to college, including the most prestigious schools in the nation. Members of the community worked together to improve the educational system and help students achieve their goals of a college education.

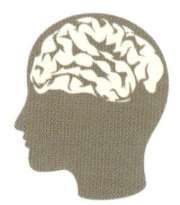

Western Medicine versus Alternative Medicine

Western medicine—the kind that most doctors practice in North America and Europe—is primary focused on addressing and trying to prevent disease. It looks at diet, exercise, prescription drugs, and surgical procedures as a way to prevent disease. It believes that diseases are caused by things from outside the body, such as viruses, bacteria, and poor nutrition.

Meanwhile, alternative medicine often has a different idea of what it means to be healthy. Health is often seen as a balance of energies within the body. Many alternative medical practices focus on a more holistic view of medicine, one that includes everything from diet, relationships, lifestyle choices, spirituality, and emotions. These alternative forms of medicine are often rooted in cultural traditions, whether Asian or Native American.

Today more and more traditional Western doctors encourage their patients to combine Western and alternative medical practices. These doctors believe some aspects of alternative medicine can be useful in supplementing a Western health-care plan.

After graduating from Dartmouth, Lori traveled cross-country to attend Stanford University School of Medicine in California. After graduation, she did a general surgery residency at Stanford University Hospital. In 1994, she became the first Navajo woman to earn board certification in surgery.

After completing her medical education, Lori went to work for the Indian Health Service. They assigned her to the Gallup Medical Center in Gallup, New Mexico, where she treated members of the Navajo and Zuni tribes. She often thought, however, that though she was a good surgeon, she was not a good healer. She sought the advice of the healers of her tribe. They reminded her that there is a connection between everything in life. There is a bond between human

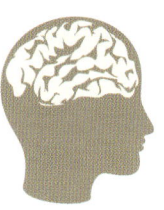

beings, the spirit, and nature, and to be healthy, there needs to be **synchrony** between all.

Navajo healers bring together symbols, music, and ceremonies to aid the process of getting well. Family and friends have important roles as well. Lori has tried to incorporate some of those into her practice. She works closely with other health-care personnel as well as patient families to incorporate aspects of the patient's cultural history and experiences to achieve the best outcome. To Lori, hospitals should have plenty of windows and trees outside, animals nearby, and attractive smells and sounds. The goal is to soothe, and anything that is harsh or causes stress should be avoided in the hospital environment.

As of 2008, Lori divided her time between her practice in New Mexico and Dartmouth University Medical School, where, in 1997, she accepted an assistant professor position and became the associate dean for student and multicultural affairs. She continues to be a role model to her people—and to all women.

Words to Know

Prestigious: Important or well-known.
Ivy League: one of a group of socially prestigious universities in the Northeastern United States, having a reputation for high academic achievement.
Diverse: varied, containing many different kinds of people or things.
Synchrony: the relationship that exists when things happen at the same time.

Find Out More

Alvord, Lori Arviso. *The Scalpel and the Silver Bear*. New York: Bantam, 2000.

Changing the Face of Medicine: Dr. Lori Arviso Alvord
www.nlm.nih.gov/changingthefaceofmedicine/physicians/biography_7.html.

Frazier, Ian. *On the Rez*. New York: Picador, 2001.

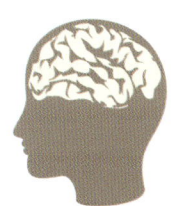

11

Opportunities for Women Today in the Field of Medicine

The medical profession hasn't always been friendly toward women, as you can see. Luckily, many women have always wanted to be doctors, and they have overcome the odds to practice medicine.

Actually, during most of history, women had a big role to play in healing. Women often treated sickness, helped other women give birth, and generally made people more comfortable. It was only more recently that people started to think that only men were fit to be doctors and healers.

More and more young woman are entering medical schools and becoming doctors.

Today, however, women are once more proving that they excel in the world of medicine. After being kept out of medical schools and hospitals for decades, more and more women today are joining the ranks of doctors. There are plenty of opportunities for interested women to become doctors.

Medical School

Women now make up almost half of all medical school graduates. In 2011 in the United States, 48.3 percent—almost half—of students who graduated from medical school were women. That's a lot of progress from the past, when women weren't allowed to attend medical schools. Most of those female graduates go on to get residencies, too. Also in 2011, about 45 percent of medical residents were women.

In Canada, women actually make up more than half of all medical students. Women received 57.1 percent of all the medical degrees earned in 2011. In fact, the first time female graduates outnumbered male graduates was in 1996.

Though some women may face some discrimination from time to time, it looks like things are getting better. It has become normal for women to get a medical education. Seeing a woman in a medical class or on rotation is a normal part of health care.

Working as a Doctor

The numbers of female doctors are lower than female medical school students, but that doesn't mean things aren't changing. The trend of women in medicine is pretty new. There are still many more older male doctors than older female doctors. As more older doctors retire, and younger ones take their place, more doctors will be women. In 2011, 33.8 percent of physicians and surgeons were women, but that number is growing every year.

Some specialties attract women more than others. The top five specialties for women in 2010 were internal medicine, pediatrics, general and family medicine, obstetrics and gynecology, and psychiatry. You'll find more women doctors in these departments than others.

Doctor-Teacher

Doctors have a few choices when it comes to jobs. Most doctors work in offices or hospitals. Some work at medical schools as well. They want to teach the next generation of medical care professionals.

During the 2009–2010 school year, women made up 36 percent of medical faculty members. That's about the same percent of women in medicine in general. Just like with doctors, numbers will probably grow as more older male faculty retire. There will be lots of opportunities for women to join medical schools.

Overcoming Further Challenges

Things are looking up for women who want to be doctors, or who are already. However, they still face some challenges. Despite more acceptance of female

Opportunities in the Field of Medicine

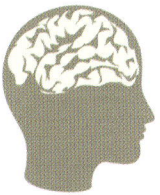

doctors, not everyone feels completely positive about it. One doctor even wrote an article titled "Are There Too Many Female Medical Graduates? Yes" in the *British Medical Journal*. The author argues that women do not contribute as much to the medical profession as men. Clearly, some people still aren't comfortable with women as doctors.

Some professionals complain that women are not as fit to be doctors because they have children. Mothers have to take time away from their jobs to have and raise children, which some people see as a bad thing. Other people, though, argue that it doesn't matter because most female doctors come back to work after having children. And some people say that maybe we should think about allowing men to share in having time off to raise children. Why should parenting be only the woman's job?

Even though women still face some challenges as doctors, things are getting better. More women, and men, realize that everyone can be a good doctor, if they are willing to put in the hard work and long years it takes to become one. You'll be seeing more and more women at the doctor's office and hospital as time goes on.

It takes hard work to become a doctor—but most women doctors find it was well worth the effort!

Find Out More

Boulis, Ann K. and Jerry A. Jacobs. *The Changing Face of Medicine: Women Doctors and the Evolution of Health Care in America*. Cornell, N.Y.: ILR Press, 2010.

Catalyst: Women in Medicine
www.catalyst.org/knowledge/women-medicine.

American Academy of Ophthalmology, "From Past to Present: The Changing Demographics of Women in Medicine"
www.aao.org/yo/newsletter/200806/article04.cfm.

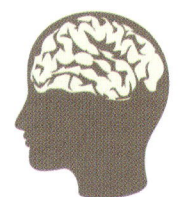

Index

Africa 49
American Medical Association (AMA) 5, 13, 29, 37–40
anthropology 6, 17

Belgium 17
biology 6, 11, 17–18, 24, 32, 39, 52, 54

Canada 21–23, 32, 47, 60
chemistry 6, 11, 26
Cohen, Stanley 18
Curie, Marie 26

Federal Bureau of Investigation (FBI) 33

genetics 22–24
Germany 25

Hong Kong 47–50

Japan 22

Mussolini, Benito 17

nephrology 42, 45
neurology 5, 17, 19
Nobel, Alfred 18
Nobel Prize 15–16, 18, 26, 28–29

pathology 5, 24, 32–35
Pearl Harbor 22, 27
pediatrics 11, 13, 24, 37, 42–43, 61
physics 6, 26–28
physiology 16–18, 29
psychiatry 11, 17, 42, 61
Puerto Rico 41–42

Rome 18

zoology 17

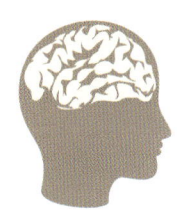

About the Author & Consultant

Kim Etingoff lives in Boston, Massachusetts, spending part of her time working on farms. Kim has written a number of books for young people on topics including health, history, nutrition, and business.

Ann Lee-Karlon, PhD, is the President of the Association for Women in Science (AWIS) in 2014–2016. AWIS is a national non-profit organization dedicated to advancing women in science, technology, engineering, and mathematics. Dr. Lee-Karlon also serves as Senior Vice President at Genentech, a major biotechnology company focused on discovering and developing medicines for serious diseases such as cancer. Dr. Lee-Karlon holds a BS in Bioengineering from the University of California at Berkeley, an MBA from Stanford University, and a PhD in Bioengineering from the University of California at San Diego, where she was a National Science Foundation Graduate Research Fellow. She completed a postdoctoral fellowship at the University College London as an NSF International Research Fellow. Dr. Lee-Karlon holds several U.S. and international patents in vascular and tissue engineering.

Picture Credits

p. 8: Ron Chapple (Dreamstime); p. 11: Lisa F. Young (Dreamstime); pp. 14, 16: Torino Scienza; p. 20: Vaneullus Foto; p. 28: National Academy of Sciences; p. 30: Jakub Jirsak (Dreamstime); p. 33: Luchschen (Dreamstimes); p. 36: University of Buffalo; p. 40: U.S. Government; p. 44: New York State Archives; p. 48: World Economic Forum; p. 52: (c) emeagwali.com; p. 60: Fototastic

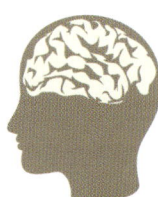